READY WRITERS

TIPS FOR YOUR VISION

Printed in the United States of America

G-Level Multimedia

Blood Drop Inheritance Group

First Printing: May 2021

ISBN - 9798507212361

ACKNOWLEDGEMENTS

This gift from God has graced me with has been and is an incredible journey is one that is to be shared with those who may also have a vision of the power of words. He has made it all possible and I am continually humbled and in awe of this honor.

God has enlisted an uncommon mentor, Dr. Cheryl A. Hill, founder of G-Level, Christians In The Marketplace, to constantly develop and push me to produce. She has taken time to assist with the compilation of all of this information for others to produce their vision.

I will always be forever grateful and give honor to my Pastor Elaine W. Green, who God allowed to see and activate this gift in me. I pray that the fruit of her labor continues to manifest as she watches with the great cloud of witnesses from the heavenly realm.

PREFACE

Get started writing your first book. If you are seeking strategies and understanding that do not require intensive studies, this is the book for you. If you are a first-time author, you're probably nervous about this decision and you want your book to be a success the first time. It can be overwhelming and costly if you do not have the right information. For this purpose, I have written this brief but informational book to help ease some of your brief anxiety.

If you're ready to jump in the water, **become an author** and learn how to write your book and get it published, you have purchased the right book.

This journey of writing your first book can be the most challenging but rewarding experience of your life.

It starts first with what you believe.

I am honored to share several tips that I have learned throughout my experience as an Author, so that you can go on to become an Author and continue to share your gift of storytelling with many people around the world.

Here's how to write a book step-by-step:

1. **<u>Develop an Author's mindset</u>**
2. **<u>Determine your book's topic</u>**
3. **<u>Create a book outline</u>**
4. **<u>Finish writing your manuscript</u>**
5. **<u>Edit your book</u>**
6. **<u>Choose a compelling book cover</u>**
7. **<u>Format your book</u>**
8. **<u>Prepare to launch your book</u>**
9. **<u>Publish your book</u>**
10. **<u>Market your book</u>**

CHAPTER ONE

Your Basic Mindset

Whatever you believe you will do. The "basic" tip or step in this journey is to "believe in yourself". Success begins with what you see or visualize.

We will discuss how to develop an Author's mindset and how to produce your thought from your thoughts to paper.

Tips for success as you write a book:

1. Develop an author's mindset. This is all about embracing a mentality that will inspire you to start and finish writing your book.

2. Strategy for writing. This step determines how you will write. Will it be a documentary, autobiography, fiction, non-fiction, etc. Once determined you will know how to proceed. There are many options for each genre. This key is to help you to understand the direction in which you are to proceed.

Step #1 – Develop a Writer's Mindset

Writing a book takes time, work, and dedication. Many people have the gift/skill to write but they do not "dedicate" the time to stay on course to write the book. Dreaming about something remains a dream until you task yourself to a date and time to get to the finish line.

Let's take the "first step" and decide that you will take the time to write your book for the next three months (if necessary). Schedule a date and time that is consistent so that you will create a habit. This schedule will cause you to at a minimum concentrate on producing thoughts on paper. A writer cannot be forced to write but you can create a habit of concentration and create a time of purpose.

Here are three things that will add to the success of your "start-time". The moment you put your first thoughts to paper…you have succeeded. Creating a writer's habit:

#1 – Holds You Accountable to Writing Your Book.

There will be times when you will not feel the flow of thoughts to write but in many cases, the "habit" of concentration creates a fresh look for you to develop different days where writing is the last thing you want to be doing.

Here's a good recipe for setting your goals:

1. **Set a writing goal**. Determine a <u>**writing goal**</u> to include a date and time each week to write. Set a deadline date. Each person's flow of creativity is different. This creates a pattern for your creative juices to flow.

2. **Set a word count goal.** Consider how many words you want to write each week. This helps you to bite off chunks of your book. You can use the <u>**Word Count Calculator** to help you.</u>

3. **Go for it!** Write what you feel and correct it later!

My greatest time of creativity is early in the morning around 5:00 a.m. I may spend two to three hours writing and then carry on with my day. I write early in the morning before I do anything else for 1-2 hours. I find that as I go throughout the day and work on other projects my mind isn't as fresh or sharp by the end of the day.

As a new author, many people "get stuck" by thinking about all of the challenges that they might face instead of starting. Join the club. These are normal thought processes but you will overcome them! Acknowledge your feelings and jump in the water and let's swim!

Wisdom Keys for your initial start:

1. **Pray first.** Your spirit and soul (how you think) must be at peace and you must be able to be able to flow in thought. I take time to pray daily, not only to write but to center my thoughts for my day.

2. **Get inspired**. Who can you glean from as a writer? Read something about this person so that you will know that you too are able to achieve success. Learn their processes, challenges, and tips.

3. **Give yourself some slack**. Each step that you achieve is a success. Accept each step and stay on your path of success.

4. **Use positive affirmations**. What you say you will have. Practice the pattern of positive thoughts. You can read books, listen to audios or repeat positive quotes.

#2 – Make An Announcement

When you take your dream from your "headspace" and audibly announce it to others, this will set you in a place of accountability. This forces you to set a goal. You should get an accountability partner to check your process. Talking with someone else at times releases thoughts and gives you a "dumping place" to walk out your visions. Take time to have a coffee break and dump your ideas and enjoy your accountability partner. They may be able to trigger your creativity. I have a couple of people that are great at pushing me and triggering my storylines. One person, in particular, is very good at details and intrigue. Because I write Christian dramas and children's novels, a person such as Camille who is passionate and vision savvy helps me to flow in my thoughts when writing. She and I have regular check-ins about the characters of my book.

CHAPTER TWO

Choose a Book Writing Software

Your next step in how to write a book has to do with **writing tools**.

Nowadays, we have everything that we need at our disposal. The internet has become our useful "assistant". You can find an endless assortment of useful **book writing software** to help you be an efficient and effective writer. If you are writing a novel you may be interested in **novel writing software or requirements** for writing a manuscript, uploading a book, etc.

The truth is that the right tools and even **self-publishing companies** make writing and publishing easier and more enjoyable.

Here are a few free resources that may help you create structure and ease of writing.

- **Google Drive**

  - You can organize all aspects of your project in folders (research, outline, manuscript drafts, etc.)
  - You can host files for your projects like images, photos, etc.

- You can use Google Docs as a word processor.

- You can enable **offline access** and work on your files even when you don't have an internet connection, such as when you're traveling.

- You can collaborate easily with others, avoiding version control issues.

- You can access it from just about any device (laptop, smartphone, tablet, you name it).

If you have a Gmail account, you have a Google Drive account.

● <u>Grammarly</u>

This is my favorite "go-to". *Grammarly* is an editing tool that helps you identify grammatical errors, typos, and incorrect sentence structure in your writing.

Download the web extension and Grammarly will edit almost anything you type in a web browser. https://www.grammarly.com/

● <u>Evernote</u>

Inspiration can strike at any time. Capture those thoughts and ideas as they happen in Evernote. You can even sync **<u>Google Drive and Evernote</u>**. You can also put this on your mobile device.

- **A Notebook & Pen**

I love to write as well as type. When writing, it sometimes serves as a therapeutic method for me at times. When inspiration hits, your paper and pen will have

Even if you write your entire manuscript on a trusty **writing software program**, you'll still want to have a dedicated notebook available for the times when inspiration strikes and you can't access a computer.

Every writer should have a notebook handy for random ideas and thoughts. You can jot these down in your notebook, then revisit them and digitally store them in your book writing software when you're back at the computer.

CHAPTER THREE

Determine Your Book Topic

It all starts with an idea. What's your **book idea**?

This is where it will be important to do a bit of research, depending on what you will write about. You may already know your topic and you can proceed.

Your first book should be written on something you know or by something that you are strongly inspired by. Use these writing prompts to help you to identify what you are passionate about.

This works whether you are writing a non-fiction how-to guide or a fictional novel. You will need to attract and connect emotionally with your targeted audience.

Here are a few key tips to accomplish this task:

● **Identify your target reader**

When you understand where you are going, it becomes easier to move forward. The key to producing meaningful content is understanding your target reader. This can be done by developing a reader persona. This is a fictional representation of your ideal audience.

To get started with your reader persona, consider answering the following questions:

1. **What's the reader's age?** Are you writing a self-help book geared towards mature adults, or are you writing a guide for teenagers? The age of your reader will set the tone for your writing and the book's context.

2. **What's the reader's education level?** Are you writing a book for children, faith leaders, or corporate leadership? Depending on the answer, your writing style, verbiage, and word choice will vary.

3. **Does the reader prefer visuals?** Think about your book's potential topic and if visuals like charts, graphs, tables, **<u>illustrations</u>**, screenshots, or photographs will be expected.

4. **What is this reader interested in?** When you write a book, it's less about what you want to say, and more about what your reader needs to know. As you start to brainstorm a topic and write your book, always have a reader-focused approach.

When you set out to write a book, you have to think about your reader wants to know more than what you want to say. Make your book about the reader: what do they need to know in order to learn what you have to say?

My main audience is children, faith leaders, and fiction novels. This focuses on biblical truths in spiritual and practical ways. These readers are interested in how to apply biblical truths to their everyday lifestyle. This is a key focus when I am writing.

● Write about something that intrigues you

You need to write about something that sparks your curiosity, something that keeps you coming back day after day. Something that you are passionate about!

This is paramount. If you choose a topic to write about for the wrong reason, you will not have an interesting read. Your readers will be able to detect your passion through your words.

You need to be able to stick with it through dry spells and bouts of non-inspiration. Your own desire to hear the story will be what drives you through.

● Research and develop topic lines

In our digital age, we can conveniently research topics from the comfort of our own home.

Google makes it easy to **research** just about any topic. Have multiple ideas for your book? Search on Google to learn more.

Here is a shortcut and informational basis that can be used to justify your book title:

- **What content already exists?** Are there already books written on this topic? If so, which ones performed well? Why did they perform well? Is there anything interesting about their content that enhanced the reader's experience? Is the market over-saturated on this topic? If it is a drama/non-fiction, who has a similar story?

- **What experts are using the same platform or idea?** Are there well-known authors on this topic? Who are they? What can you learn from them?

- **What can you glean and use?** Are there specific things you need to learn to create an interesting good read (ex. geography, culture, time period, true story, etc.)?

I performed extensive research before writing the manuscript for Inbound Content. It was important for me to understand what content was already out there, which content was performing well, and most importantly, how could I make my book unique. This is exactly why I included homework after each chapter to help my readers build an action plan that they could implement immediately, something I noticed wasn't typical in other marketing books.

- **Choose a topic where you can infuse your experience and write about it quickly**

This will be important for your *first book only*. Your first writing will be your prototype and provide you the "experience" of writing and getting what you write published. It is "completing this first process" that provides to you your success because you will also learn your strengths and endurance abilities. You should not get stuck on a topic unless you know that this is a topic that you must write about. Again, choose a topic or experience that you can write about quickly, with limited resources.

Here's how to find a topic you can write about quickly. Take time to write down the following:

1. **Write what you can teach right now.** If you had to teach a lesson on something right at this second, what could you teach on with ease? This is a topic you know well, that requires limited additional research, and what you can quickly create content for.

2. **Write about a powerful experience.** Each individual is unique in their experiences. Everyone has gone through something that changed them. Reflect on your life and think about one experience that sticks out about your life.

3. **Write about a life lesson.** What have you experienced that can of value to others? What are the life lessons?

CHAPTER FOUR

Write A Book Outline

Now that you are finding a strategic road map to move forward, write it down and begin to schedule a time to develop a strategy around the topic or experience.

One leader said "If you want something that you never had, you have to do something that you have never done"- Mike Murdock.

As it has been said over the years, "getting started requires participation"-Dr. Cheryl A. Hill

Let's review what you can do to create a clear **book outline** for your book that you can use as a roadmap.

#1 – Create a Mindmap

A mindmap is a simple way of creating a strategy. Once you have your idea of your title, you have your direction. Now it is time to target how to address and to get the information out. With a mindmap, you can drill your topic down into sub-topics. It will help you get all of your ideas out and onto paper.

Here are a few steps that I learned that will help you with your book's topic:

1. Get a blank piece of paper and pen.
2. Set a timer for 10 minutes.
3. Write your topic in the middle of the page.
4. Jot down all of your ideas related to your book's topic.
5. Do not stop writing until the timer goes off.

Once you have **mind-mapped your idea**, you should have a full page of brainstormed thoughts, ideas, and concepts. You can then review what you've written, and begin to organize them. This will come in handy when it comes time to actually start plugging in content for your book outline.

#2 – Write a Purpose Statement

In one sentence describe the purpose of your book. A strong purpose statement will explain to readers **why** they should consider reading your book.

This will also help you stay focused as you begin drafting your outline and writing your book. It will prevent you from straying from related topics.

When you have trouble solidifying **what your book is about**, review your *purpose statement.*

Example: Stolen Property: **People who read this book will experience the supernatural adventure of children from a Christian perspective. Her vision will intrigue and captivate the reader's imagination into the mysteries.**

#3 – Create a Working Title

A working title is a *temporary title* used during the production of your book. Identifying your book by giving it a name can help set the direction.

This allows you to revisit the title as you continue to develop your story. You should not get "stuck" on the title in the beginning. Your imagination will take time to reach your "paper". You may start with one idea but as you continue to write, your creativity will lead you. A working title is just that, a title being worked on.

#4 – Draft a Working Outline For Your Book

Get excited! You are doing great. Once you reach this process, you are ready to work and track your progress. You now have a better vision or roadmap of how to structure your time. The outline can change throughout your writing process and that is absolutely fine!

If you want to create a solid foundation for your book in just a few hours, consider **this BookMap method**. It's a template you can follow to quickly pull together all the subjects you want to write about and organize them into topics that will become chapters of your book.

Your outline will do wonders for you once you start writing. It can help you **avoid writer's block**, and increase your writing momentum and **productivity**. Instead of wondering what to write about in the next chapter of your book, you'll already have an idea of where to start with your book's outline.

#6 – Fill In The Gaps With More Research

After your working outline is completed, it's important to do further research on your topic so that you can fill in any areas that you missed or forgot to include in your original outline.

Research is important, but writing is more important when it comes to completing your book. So, make sure you balance time for research wisely.

Do not get too caught up in **your research** that it prevents you from writing your book. Take some time to research, but set a limit. Always go back to writing.

Here's how to research when writing a book:

1. Use online resources by doing a Google search on your topic.
2. Read other books that have been written about your topic.

3. Listen to expert interviews, podcasts, and audiobooks related to your topic.

4. Read scholarly articles and academic journals within the subject or industry.

5. Search archives, collections, historical journals, data records, and newspaper clippings to get clear on events, dates, and facts about your topic, especially if you're writing about the past.

#7 – *Frameworks On How To Write Your Book*

If your book can follow a framework, this will make it easier to keep your writing organized and relevant.

By choosing a format or structure for your book's topic, you'll be able to align your outline in a way that will be helpful when you start to write each chapter.

Most **nonfiction books** can fall into a specific framework or a blend of frameworks. It's better to start with a specific framework, then tweak it as needed as you continue writing.

Here are common nonfiction book frameworks to consider when writing a book:

1. **Modular:** Use this framework if you have a lot of information or concepts that can be grouped into similar topics, but don't need to be presented in a specific order.

2. **Reference:** Use this framework if your book will be used as a reference that makes it easy for readers to quickly find the information they need.

3. **Three Act Structure:** Use this framework if you plan to use storytelling in your book, where you have three main parts like a Set-Up, Rising Action, and Resolution.

4. **Sequential:** Use this framework if your book reads like a "how-to" with a specific set of steps.

5. **Compare & Contrast:** Use this framework if you need to show your reader how two or more ideas or concepts are similar to or different from one another.

6. **Problem & Solution:** Use this framework if readers need to be able to clearly identify a problem and understand the solution.

7. **Chronological:** Use this framework if each main section of your book represents a specific time or order of events.

8. **Combination:** If your book will fall under two or more of the above frameworks, then you will need to use a combination framework that's adjusted to your book's specific topic.

CHAPTER FIVE

Finish Writing Your Book Draft

For many, the hard part isn't getting started with how to write a book… it's in **finishing it**!

Commit to finishing your first draft, and you're already succeeding!

Here are our top tips to keep the momentum going as you start taking action after learning exactly how to write a book.

#1 – Break your book writing into small chunks

Now that you have your book's outline and framework, it's time to get started with writing.

Like a marathon, your manuscript is essentially a puzzle made up of many smaller like-themed pieces. Your finished book maybe 262 pages long, but it's written one word or thought at a time. Pace yourself and stick to your **consistent writing schedule**.

If you approach your book writing by focusing too much on the larger picture, you can get overwhelmed. Write chapter-by-chapter.

Related: **How to Write a Book Chapter in 7 Simple Steps**

Start with baby steps by chunking your writing into small pieces. Set milestones, and celebrate the small wins.

Here are some tips for breaking your writing into small pieces:

1. **Write one chapter at a time**. Focus on one piece at a time, not the entire puzzle!

2. **Set deadlines to complete each chunk of writing**. Break your goal down into smaller sections, then set individual deadlines for each section.

3. **Structure your writing time**. Follow a **routine for writing** that includes time for research (if needed) and review. For example, if you dedicate two hours each day towards your book, set 30 minutes aside to review your outline so you know what you're writing about, then 30 minutes to research anything that you need to clarify, then one hour to actually writing.

4. **Celebrate small goals**. As you accomplish milestones towards your end goal, schedule and celebrate your small accomplishments. It can be something as simple as going out to dinner, buying yourself a small gift, or doing a little dance.

*Pro tip: Set deadlines to complete the chunks of writing you need to **meet your goal**. This will help you better prioritize your blocks of writing time and word count goal.*

#2 – Build the momentum to finish writing your book

Writing is difficult. Writing an entire book is even more difficult.

When you're in the weeds with writing your book, there will be days you want to give it all up.

There will also be times when you have writer's block, and even though you know what you should be writing about, it all sounds wrong as you re-read what you've written in your head.

Here's how to fight writer's block and increase your writing momentum:

1. **Don't edit as you write**. Writing and editing require your brain to work in two very different ways, so don't do it! It'll slow you down, and keep you at a standstill. Keep writing, and save the editing for later. It's okay if what you type out doesn't sound perfect; it's all about getting your words out first. You can clean them up later.

2. **Switch up your scenery.** If you usually write at home in your own writing space, maybe it's time to freshen up your writing environment. Try writing in a public park, or at a

coffee shop or library on the days when writing is the last thing you feel like doing.

3. **Take a break.** It's okay if you're too mentally worn-out to write. Take a small break, and then get back to it. When we say small break, we mean take a day or two off from writing (not a month or two!).

4. **Get creative inspiration elsewhere.** Binge-watch an exciting new show, read a novel, take a walk in nature, go to an art gallery, or be around people you love. While you aren't writing when you do these things, it can help your brain reset and recharge so you can return to your book.

5. **Write about something else.** Sometimes, when we're so engulfed in our book's topic, it can be self-limited. If you're feeling less excited about writing when it comes to your book, maybe it's time to flex your writing muscles differently. Try doing some **creative writing exercises**, journal, or write a poem.

#3 – Collaborate with others

There's strength in numbers when it comes to accomplishing a huge task.

And, more importantly, it can help you feel less isolated in what can be a very solitary act. Writing a book can be lonely!

Let's review three things you can do to collaborate with others when writing your book.

#1 – Connect with your original accountability partner or group

A great example of finding accountability partners is through a group or self-publishing company much like what **Self-Publishing School** does with their Mastermind Community on Facebook.

#2 – Attend a writer's conference

Sharing space and networking with other writers can do wonders for your writing habits and momentum. By attending **writer's conferences**, you'll be in a room full of people just like you.

Not only will you be able to network with and learn from expert authors who have been where you are, but you'll also be able to meet fellow aspiring writers going through the same process as you.

#3 Bring Your Book to the Finish Line

Now it's time to put on your **marketing** pants and spread the word about your book!

CHAPTER SIX

Include Front & Back Matter

There are elements outside of your book's content that you'll need to write, such as a preface, foreword, notes, etc. I suggest waiting until **after** you've written your book. This way, not only can you better connect them to your story, but you won't waste time editing them in case you make changes to your manuscript.

Let's review eight final touches you may or may not need to wrap up your book.

#1 – Preface or Introduction

Draw in your readers with a compelling story. This could be a personal anecdote related to your topic. Tell them what the book is about and why it is relevant to them (think of your reader persona from earlier).

#2 – Foreword

A foreword is typically written by another author or thought leader of your particular industry. Getting someone credible to write this can add a lot of value to your readers.

#3 – Testimonials

Just like with the foreword, try and find respected, well-known people in your space and have them write a review about your book. The best way to promote yourself is to have someone else speak on your behalf.

#4 – Author Bio

How do you want to be portrayed to your audience? Readers love knowing personal details of an author's life, such as your hobbies, where you live, or what inspired you to write this book.

*Pro tip: The **author bio** on the flap of your book might be one of the first things people read when deciding whether or not to read our book. Keep it short, but make sure it packs a punch (just like your elevator pitch).*

#5 – Glossary

A glossary is an alphabetical list of terms or words relating to a specific subject, text, or dialect with corresponding explanations. If you are writing nonfiction, especially a topic that uses a lot of lingo or uncommon words, make sure to include a glossary to create a better experience for your readers.

#6 – Notes

If you are **<u>writing nonfiction</u>**, keep track of your sources as you research and write. A clear bibliography will only add to your value and credibility.

Being nonfiction that was based on a lot of research and experiments, I made sure to include a notes section in Inbound Content. It included citations, stats, image sources, etc.

Time To Edit Your Book

Once your manuscript is completed, it's time to edit your book, which involves self-editing first, then having a thorough professional edit done.

The success of your book will depend on its quality, and a thoroughly edited book is a solid way to increase your book's quality.

Even the best writers require editing, so don't feel discouraged by this process. In the end, you'll be glad you followed the editing process and will have a completed, error-free book that you can be proud of.

#1– Self-edit your book

Remember when we told you not to edit your book as you wrote? Well, now's your time to shine in the editing department.

Once your book is written, it's time to go through and read it line-by-line.

We recommend printing your entire manuscript out on paper, then going through each page and making edits. This will make it easy to spot errors and will help you easily implement these changes into your manuscript.

There's a specific strategy to **self-editing**; if you start this process blindly, it can be overwhelming, so make sure you understand how it works before diving in.

You'll want to read for structure, readability, grammar, and word choice. There are a few different ways to self-edit a book, and it will depend on your preferences.

Here are some tips to self-edit your book successfully:

1. Read your manuscript aloud as you edit.
2. Start with one chapter at a time.

3. First, go through and edit the chapter for structure revisions.

4. Second, find opportunities for improving the book's readability.

5. Third, make edits for grammar and word choice.

Once you complete your self-edit, you can make your revisions on your manuscript, then get ready for the next round of edits.

#2– Hire a professional book editor

Now, it's time to hand your book off to a professional editor.

As meticulous as you may be, there are bound to be some grammatical or spelling errors that get overlooked. Also, a professional editor should be able to give you feedback on the structure of your writing so you can feel confident in your final published draft.

Related: **Explore Line Editing vs Copyediting**

#3 – Re-write sections of your book's draft using your editor's feedback

Now it's time to improve your book using your editor's feedback. Don't be discouraged when you get your manuscript back full of edits, comments, and identified errors.

Think of these edits as opportunities to improve your book. You want to give your reader a polished, well-written book, and to do this, you need to edit and re-write.

This doesn't mean you have to re-write your entire book. You simply have to go through your editor's feedback and make any revisions you think are necessary.

If there is something you don't agree with your editor on, that's okay. In the end, it is your book, and you are in control of what you want to add or take out of the manuscript.

Just be sure your revisions are coming from a place of sound reasoning, and not pride.

#4 – Finalize your book title

If you haven't done so already, it's time to revisit the working title you created for your book earlier in the process.

You need to finalize your book's title before you move on to the next steps!

Related: **Book Title Generator**

If you need help deciding on a title, cast a vote with your target readers and mentors in your author network. Send an email out, post a **social media announcement**, or reach out through text with people that are considered your book's ideal readers.

Get feedback on your title by asking people to vote for their favorite. Include the top three choices, then use the crowdsourced results to narrow it down even more.

Once you have a title selected, don't worry too much if you're not 100 percent sold on it yet. Even if the title turns out to not be effective, you can always change the title depending on the publishing platform you select.

CHAPTER SEVEN

Choose A Compelling Book Cover

Don't judge a book by its cover? Please. **People are definitely judging your book by its cover.**

The cover design is generally the first thing that will pique a reader's interest.

Related: **Self-Publishing Services**

You can find freelance graphic designers to create a compelling book cover for you on many online marketplace sites like Upwork, **Reedsy**, and **Snappa**. You can even check with a local graphic design artist for a more hands-on approach.

Tips for creating an effective book cover:

- Whitespace is your friend. Make it a best practice to choose a design that pops, but doesn't distract.
- Make it creative (non-fiction) or emotional (fiction). Do your best to connect the art to the story or use it to enhance the title.

- Consider a subtitle. Think of this as a one-sentence descriptor of what this book is about.

- Test two or three designs. Send a few designs to your trusted accountability group to get their honest first impressions and feedback.

CHAPTER EIGHT

Format Your Book

Now that you've written your manuscript, it's time to format it so you can visualize the final product — your book!

Formatting your book is an important step because it has to do with how your book will appear for the reader. A successfully formatted book will not cut off text, incorrect indentations, or typeset errors when printed or displayed on a digital device.

If you've already decided to go with **self-publishing versus traditional publishing**, this is all on you. But if you're not tech-savvy and don't have the time to learn how to format your own book, you can hire a professional to do this part for you.

If you know **how to format a book** correctly and to fit your book distributor's specification, you can do so in Word or Google Docs. You can also use a program like **Vellum Software**.

Otherwise, we recommend hiring someone to do this professionally, as it's one of the most important aspects to get right. Check out **Formatted Books** if that's the case for you.

CHAPTER NINE

Prepare To Launch Your Book

Before you hit "Publish" it's time to do the groundwork to start prepping for your book's launch, and your ongoing book launch and **book marketing** strategy.

There are a few steps involved in this process, which we'll outline below.

#1 – Build your book's launch team

This is an ongoing step that you can start doing when you are finished with your rough draft. As you send your book to the editor, designer, and formatter, you can **organize a launch team** in the meantime.

Your book's launch team is essentially a group of individuals that are considered your target readers. They will help you promote your book, and will be actively involved in the launch process of your book.

#2 – Develop a marketing mindset

It's time to start shifting your mindset from writing to **book marketing**. Think about your strengths and areas of growth when it comes to sales and marketing.

Acknowledge any fears or self-limiting thoughts you have, then push past them by remembering your book's purpose. Know that the power of sharing your knowledge and experience through your book is stronger than any fear that might hold you back.

It's important to understand in the marketing phase that your mindset has a huge role in the success of your book. You can write the best book in the world, but if you don't channel some energy towards marketing, no one will know it exists.

#3 – Create a book launch strategy

There are a lot of moving parts when it comes to your launch strategy, so it's important to draft up a plan before you publish your book.

Your launch strategy is basically how you plan to create momentum with your book. Think of it as a business launch. There's always a big celebration to announce the launch of the business. It's the same for your book.

CHAPTER TEN

Publish Your Book

The self-publishing process steps will vary on whether you are **publishing your book as an eBook** only, or whether you plan to **publish it as a print book.**

It will also vary depending on which **self-publishing companies** you plan to work with. There are many self-publishing platforms to choose from, including **Amazon's KDP** and **IngramSpark**.

If you plan to work with a different **book publisher**, you'll want to follow their guidelines.

Once you've hit publish on your platform, you can start implementing your launch strategies and marketing strategies, which we'll cover in the next section.

About The Author

Becky DeWitt is an author and coach who works with authors of all genres to help them become bestselling authors. She has written and self-published over 21 titles, in different genres of contemporary fiction, inspirational, and children's books. Becky's writings reveal trial and tribulations from the ordinary everyday perspective as well as edification for the soul.

Becky is the Founder and President of The Blood Drop Inheritance Group, a group that assists emerging authors with formatting and preparing their books for publication. BDIG was created to showcase the anointing of those that God leads her to assist in the publishing process.

Becky combines her vast leadership expertise with her depth of spiritual understanding to reveal life-transforming messages that empower and inspire. She keeps the reader on the edge of their seat and opens the understanding of each reader to drama, suspense, and the godly supernatural.

Becky is also an ordained Minister, movie scriptwriter, community leader, thought leader, and an Honorary Ambassador for the G-Level Christian Marketplace Leaders Group. Becky has

delivered keynote addresses at writers conferences in the United States and has also participated at regional and national book fairs.

 She has written feature articles for various websites and print publications and her books are available on Amazon. Some have been translated into French and Spanish. The vision of her company Blood Drop Inheritance Group is to pen those words of inspiration and revelation from the throne room for all generations.

http://www.bdig-beckydewitt.org/
https://www.beckydewittglobal.org/

http://www.authorsden.com/beckydewitt

bloodropinheritance@gmail.com

Books By Becky

The Destiny's Closet Series

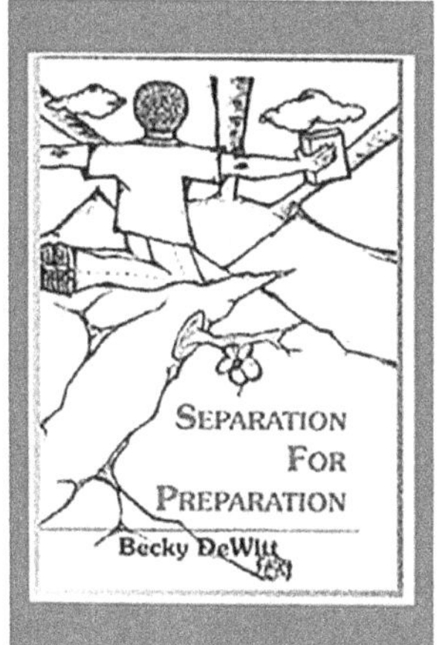

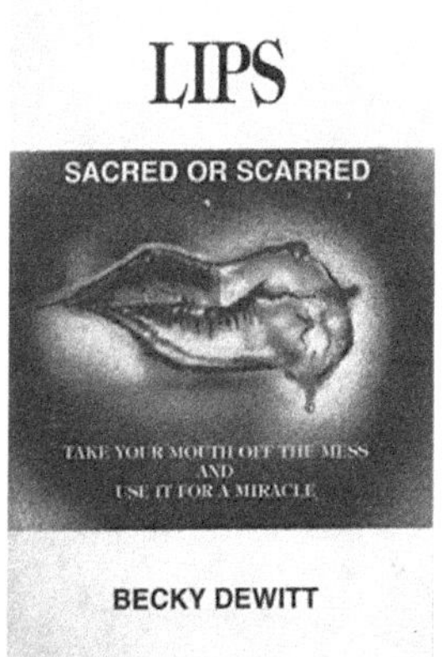

Available on
amazon

BECKY DEWITT